SUPER
SANDCASTLE
State Stories

THE
SUNSHINE CHAMPS

~ A Story About Florida ~

Written by Karen Latchana Kenney
Illustrated by Bob Doucet

Consulting Editor, Diane Craig, M.A./Reading Specialist

ABDO
Publishing Company

Published by ABDO Publishing Company
8000 West 78th Street, Edina, Minnesota 55439.

Editor: Pam Price
Content Developer: Nancy Tuminelly
Cover and Interior Design:
    Anders Hanson, Mighty Media
Photo Credits: iStockphoto (Laurent Nicolaon,
Clayton Sharrard), One Mile Up,
John Cancalosi/Peter Arnold, Shutterstock,
Quarter-dollar coin image from the United States Mint.

Library of Congress Cataloging-in-Publication Data

Kenney, Karen Latchana.
  The sunshine champs : a story about Florida / Karen
Latchana Kenney ; Illustrated by Bob Doucet.
    p. cm. -- (Fact & fable. State stories)
  ISBN 978-1-60453-187-9
  1. Florida--Juvenile literature. I. Doucet, Bob, ill. II. Title.

  F311.3.K46 2009
  975.9--dc22
                          2008019355

Super SandCastle™ books are created by a team of
professional educators, reading specialists, and content
developers around five essential components—phonemic
awareness, phonics, vocabulary, text comprehension,
and fluency—to assist young readers as they develop
reading skills and strategies and increase their general
knowledge. All books are written, reviewed, and leveled
for guided reading, early reading intervention, and
Accelerated Reader® programs for use in shared, guided,
and independent reading and writing activities to
support a balanced approach to literacy instruction.

TABLE OF CONTENTS

Map
3

Story:
The Sunshine Champs
4

Florida at a Glance
20

What Do You Know?
21

What to Do in Florida
22

Glossary
24

FLORIDA

Pensacola

Tallahassee

Jacksonville
(pg. 4)

Gainesville

oranges
(pg. 7)

St. Augustine
(pg. 8)

Daytona Beach
(pg. 11)

Shelly
the turtle
(pg. 9)

Orlando

Penny the
porpoise
(pg. 15)

Tampa
(pg. 14)

sabal palm
(pg. 17)

Port
St. Lucie

Ft. Meyers

Naples

SUNSHINE
STATE
CHAMPS

Miami
(pg. 18)

Florida Keys
(pg. 19)

LEGEND

☆ CAPITAL   ⬤ STORY START

○ CITY   ╌ ╌ STORY PATH

〰 RIVER   ✳ STORY END

Jacksonville

Jacksonville is the largest city in Florida. The St. Johns River runs through it. Jacksonville has many parks and beaches.

THE SUNSHINE CHAMPS

Alex could see the twinkling lights of the city out his bedroom window. He was packing for his big trip tomorrow. Finally, the Sunshine State Junior League Baseball Tournament was about to begin! His team, the Jacksonville Gators, lost last year. But Alex was hoping their luck would change.

Alex was a bit worried. "I know I haven't been hitting too well lately. I just have to keep trying," Alex told himself. He tossed and turned in bed that night. He was too excited to sleep. Alex hoped the Jacksonville Gators would win the tournament.

Alligator

The American alligator is the Florida state reptile. These cold-blooded, scaly creatures live in swampy, wet areas. They have strong jaws and many sharp teeth.

Panther

The panther is Florida's state animal. This large wildcat is an endangered animal. There are thought to be only 80 to 100 Florida panthers alive today.

The next morning, Alex arrived at the team bus early. His best friend, Pedro, came running over. Pedro was the only panther and the best player on the team. "Hey, Alex, are you ready for the big game tonight?" Pedro asked.

"You bet I am, Pedro!" Alex said.

The team's spirits were high as they climbed onto the bus. Alex saw Coach Frank and asked, "Will I be in tonight's lineup?"

"Not tonight, Alex," Coach told him, "but maybe next game!" Feeling disappointed, Alex stared out the bus window. He watched as they whizzed past the orange trees along the road.

Oranges

Oranges have been farmed in Florida since the mid-1800s. The flower of the orange is called the orange blossom. It is the Florida state flower.

7

They arrived in St. Augustine with an hour to spare before practice. Alex and Pedro walked through the narrow streets of the old city.

"Pedro, I really want to play in this tournament. Can you give me a few tips?" Alex asked.

"No problem, my friend," Pedro replied.

St. Augustine

St. Augustine is on the east coast of Florida. This city, known as the nation's oldest city, was the first town built in this country by Europeans. Many tourists visit this area and the rest of Florida each year.

8

Back at the practice field, Pedro was giving Alex advice. "Now watch the ball hit the bat."

Shelly, the team troublemaker, snapped, "Alex, why practice? You're not even playing tonight."

Alex didn't pay attention to the turtle. He knew that if he kept practicing, he would get his chance to play.

The Jacksonville Gators were playing the Miami Mockingbirds. The score was tied in the bottom of the seventh inning. Pedro was at bat with Shelly on third base. Pedro waited for the first pitch. He got a hit and Shelly scored the winning run! Everyone cheered! But there was something wrong.

Mockingbird

The state bird of Florida is the mockingbird. It can mock the songs of other birds. That is how it got its name.

Shelly was limping! Something had happened to her foot as she crossed home plate. Back on the bus, Coach Frank told Alex, "Okay, kid, at the Daytona game you can play. Shelly's on the bench for now. Just don't let us down." Alex was thrilled!

Daytona Beach

Daytona Beach is a city on the east coast of Florida. It is a popular tourist spot. It is also known for car racing. The Daytona 500 is held there every year.

At the next game of the Sunshine State Tournament, Alex was shaking. "Pedro, I'm so nervous!" Alex said.

"Just try your hardest," Pedro said calmly, "and forget about everything else."

Alex waited while Sammy batted ahead of him. "Go Sammy!" the team screamed. Then it was Alex's turn.

Sunshine State

Florida is known as the Sunshine State. This was made the state's official nickname in 1970.

Alex took a deep breath and focused on the ball. He thought back to his practice with Pedro. Pedro told him to watch the ball hit the bat. Alex tried, but the ball just whizzed by the bat. Strike one. He focused on the second pitch. This time he connected and got a hit! The Gators won by three runs. Alex was proud that he had helped the team win.

Spring Training

Major league baseball teams train, or practice, each spring. They want to be ready for the regular season. For over 100 years, many teams have found the Florida weather perfect for spring training.

Tampa

Tampa lies on the west coast of Florida. It has a large bay called Tampa Bay. Tampa Bay opens to the Gulf of Mexico.

The team arrived a day early in Tampa. There were two more games in the Sunshine State Tournament. But the team needed a break. Coach Frank took the team to the beach before practice. "This beach is awesome!" Alex said to Pedro. "Let's race to the water!"

"I win!" Pedro panted. They both looked at the sparkling ocean. Suddenly, a porpoise leapt into the sky and dove back into the waves.

Swimming closer to the beach, she said, "I'm Penny, and I can do all sorts of tricks. Watch!"

Alex and Pedro watched her jump, spin, and flip until they had to leave. "Bye, Penny!" they shouted.

Porpoise

The porpoise is also known as the dolphin. It is Florida's state saltwater mammal. When porpoises jump out of the water, it's called breaching.

Alex got another chance to play in the next game. They were up against the best team, the Zonking Zebras. One of them saw Alex shaking and shouted, "Just strike out and save us some time!" Alex focused on the ball and swung at the pitch. He hit a double! The team roared.

It was close, but the Gators won again. The Zebras were poor sports. They hid behind the palm trees and booed as Alex's team got back on their bus.

"Good job!" Pedro told Alex. "You keep getting better and better!" All that practicing was paying off, and Coach noticed too. It felt good.

Sabal Palm

The sabal palm is Florida's state tree. It is a tall palm that grows from 50 to 70 feet (15 to 21 meters) tall. The sabal palm is also called the cabbage palm.

Miami

Miami is a large city near the southern tip of Florida. It has a very warm climate. There is a big Cuban-American community in Miami.

18

The final game was in Miami the next day. The score was tied in the bottom of the seventh inning. Alex was at bat. He focused as the ball flew toward him. It looked like it was moving in slow motion. Smack! He hit a home run! The Gators were the Sunshine State Champs!

"Great job, team!" Coach Frank told them. "We've won a trip to the Keys for some fun in the sun and all the key lime pie we can eat!"

On the bus, Alex looked out the window. He thought, "Now that my hitting is better, I will work on my fielding next year!"

THE END

Sunshine Key Lime Pie

1 14-ounce can sweetened condensed milk

$2/3$ cup lime juice (from key limes if available)

1 cup whipped topping

1 premade graham cracker crust

Mix the sweetened condensed milk and the lime juice together in a bowl. Add the whipped topping a little at a time and stir until it is smooth and creamy. Pour the mixture into the crust. Put the pie in the refrigerator until the filling is firm (about 2–3 hours). Slice into 8 pieces.

Florida Keys

The Florida Keys are a special part of Florida. The Florida Keys are a group of islands connected by 42 bridges. Key lime pie is a famous dessert from this area.

FLORIDA AT A GLANCE

Abbreviation: FL

Capital:
Tallahassee

Largest city: Jacksonville
(13th-largest U.S. city)

Statehood: March 3,
1845 (27th state)

Area:
65,755 sq. mi.
(170,305 sq km)
(22nd-largest state)

Nickname:
Sunshine State

Motto: In God We Trust

State bird: mockingbird

State flower:
orange blossom

State tree:
sabal palm

State mammal:
panther

State butterfly:
zebra longwing

State song:
"The Swanee River
(Old Folks at Home)"

STATE SEAL

STATE FLAG

STATE QUARTER

The Florida quarter includes a Spanish ship like the ones the explorers used when they landed there. It also features a space shuttle and some sabal palm trees. The phrase "Gateway to Discovery" symbolizes Florida's past, present, and future.

What Do You Know?

How well do you remember the story? Match the pictures to the questions below! Then check your answers at the bottom of the page!

 **a.** porpoise

 **b.** city lights

 **c.** Shelly

 **d.** Pedro

 e. palm trees

 **f.** bus

1. What does Alex see out his bedroom window?

2. How does the team get to its games?

3. Who helps Alex practice hitting?

4. Who scored the winning run in the first game?

5. What kind of animal is Penny?

6. What did the Zonking Zebras hide behind?

What to Do in Florida

1 **PLAY IN THE OCEAN**
Pensacola Beach, Pensacola

2 **WATCH A CAR RACE**
Daytona 500,
Daytona Beach

3 **VISIT A MANATEE REFUGE**
Blue Spring State Park,
Orange City

4 **LEARN ABOUT SPACE TRAVEL**
Kennedy Space Center,
Cape Canaveral

5 **VISIT AN EXOTIC CAT SANCTUARY**
Big Cat Rescue, Tampa

6 **VISIT A BUTTERFLY PARK**
Butterfly World,
Coconut Creek

7 **BIKE WITH THE ALLIGATORS**
Shark Valley,
Everglades National Park

8 **VISIT A NOBEL PRIZE WINNER'S HOME**
Ernest Hemingway Home
& Museum, Key West

Georgia

★ Tallahassee

1

FLORIDA

Atlantic
Ocean

2

3

Gulf of Mexico

5

4

6

7

8 ⬭⬭⬭⬭⬭⬭

23

GLOSSARY

climate – the usual weather in a place.

dessert – a sweet food, such as fruit, ice cream, or pastry, served after a meal.

disappointed – feeling sad because something you hoped for didn't happen.

endangered – close to extinction.

focus – to concentrate on or pay particular attention to.

mammal – a warm-blooded animal that has hair and whose females produce milk to feed their young.

mock – to make fun of someone by copying the way he or she looks, sounds, or acts.

reptile – a cold-blooded animal, such as a snake, turtle, or alligator, that moves on its belly or on very short legs.

tourist – a person who visits a place for fun or to learn something.

tournament – a series of contests or games played to win a championship.

About SUPER SANDCASTLE™

Bigger Books for Emerging Readers
Grades K–4

Created for library, classroom, and at-home use, Super SandCastle™ books support and engage young readers as they develop and build literacy skills and will increase their general knowledge about the world around them. Super SandCastle™ books are part of SandCastle™, the leading PreK–3 imprint for emerging and beginning readers. Super SandCastle™ features a larger trim size for more reading fun.

Let Us Know

Super SandCastle™ would like to hear your stories about reading this book. What was your favorite page? Was there something hard that you needed help with? Share the ups and downs of learning to read. We want to hear from you! Send us an e-mail.

sandcastle@abdopublishing.com

Contact us for a complete list of SandCastle™, Super SandCastle™, and other nonfiction and fiction titles from ABDO Publishing Company.

www.abdopublishing.com • 8000 West 78th Street Edina, MN 55439 • 800-800-1312 • 952-831-1632 fax